First World War
and Army of Occupation
War Diary
France, Belgium and Germany

31 DIVISION
94 Infantry Brigade
Royal Scots Fusiliers
12th Battalion
1 May 1918 - 21 May 1919

WO95/2366/3

The Naval & Military Press Ltd
www.nmarchive.com
Published in association with The National Archives

Published by

The Naval & Military Press Ltd

Unit 10 Ridgewood Industrial Park,

Uckfield, East Sussex,

TN22 5QE England

Tel: +44 (0) 1825 749494

www.naval-military-press.com

www.nmarchive.com

This diary has been reprinted in facsimile from the original. Any imperfections are inevitably reproduced and the quality may fall short of modern type and cartographic standards.

Contents

Document type	Place/Title	Date From	Date To
Heading	WO95/2366-3 12 Battalion Royal Scots Fusiliers		
Heading	31st Division 94th Infy Bde 12th Bn Roy. Scots Fus. (Ayr & Lanark Yeo Bn) May 1918-May 1919 From Egypt 74 Div 229 Bde		
Heading	74th Division 229th Infy Bde 31 Div 94 Bde 12th Bn Roy. Scots Fus. May 1918 From Egypt		
War Diary		01/05/1918	31/05/1918
Heading	12th R Scots Fus. June 1918		
Heading	War Diary Of The 12th (Ayr & Lanark Yeomanry Battalion) R.S.F. June, 1918. Period : From June 1st, 1918. To June 30th 1918. Vol 4		
War Diary	In The Field	01/06/1918	30/06/1918
Heading	War Diary of 12th Bn. R. Scots Fus. for July 1918.		
Heading	War Diary. 12th (Ayr & Lanark Yeomanry) Battalion Royal Scots Fusiliers. July-1918. Volume 2		
War Diary	Map Ref Sheet No 36 A NE. Field	01/07/1918	31/07/1918
Heading	War Diary 12th (Ayr & Lanark Yeomanry) Bn. R. Scots Fusiliers. August. 1918. Volume III		
War Diary	Morbecque (Sheet 36A NE)	01/08/1918	08/08/1918
War Diary	In Support	09/08/1918	11/08/1918
War Diary	In Front Line	12/08/1918	15/08/1918
War Diary	In Support	16/08/1918	21/08/1918
War Diary	Wallon Cappell	22/08/1918	23/08/1918
War Diary	V 12 B.9.9.	24/08/1918	24/08/1918
War Diary	In Front Line	25/08/1918	27/08/1918
War Diary	In Support	28/08/1918	29/08/1918
War Diary	Divisional Reserve	30/08/1918	31/08/1918
Miscellaneous	Report On Operations 12th to 15th August, 1918, Resulting In Capture Of Vieux Berquin.	15/08/1918	15/08/1918
Miscellaneous	12 R. Scots Fus Sept 1918		
Heading	War Diary of 12th (Yeo) Bn Royal Scots Fusiliers From 1st September 1918 to 30th September 1918 (Volume IV)		
War Diary	Issued Reserve Area	01/09/1918	01/09/1918
War Diary	Fontaine Houck	02/09/1918	19/09/1918
War Diary	Bell Rest	24/09/1918	28/09/1918
War Diary		29/09/1918	30/09/1918
Heading	War Diary of 12th (Yeo) Bn R.S.F. for month of October 1918 Volume 5		
War Diary	94th Bde in Reserve	01/10/1918	06/10/1918
War Diary	94th Bde released the 93rd in the Line	06/10/1918	12/10/1918
War Diary	94th Bde In Reseve	12/10/1918	24/10/1918
War Diary	Field	25/10/1918	31/10/1918
Heading	War Diary of 12th (Yeo) Bn, Royal Scots Fus., for November 1918.		
Heading	The Gallipoli Campaign. Vol II Chapter XX The Landing as Surla		
War Diary	Field	31/10/1918	30/11/1918

Type	Description	Start	End
Heading	War Diary of 12th (Yeo) Bn. Royal Scots Fusiliers From 1st December 1918 to 31st December 1918. (Volume 13)		
War Diary		01/12/1918	31/12/1918
Heading	War Diary of 12th (Yeo) Bn. Royal Scots Fusiliers From 1st January 1919 to 31st January 1919 (Volume VIII)		
War Diary		01/01/1919	15/01/1919
War Diary		29/01/1919	31/01/1919
Heading	War Diary 12th (Yeo) Bn. Royal Scots Fusiliers From 1st February 1919 to 28th February 1919 Vol 14		
War Diary		01/02/1919	28/02/1919
Heading	War Diary of 12th (Yeo) Bn. Royal Scots Fusiliers From 1st March 1919 to 31st March 1919 Vol 16		
War Diary		01/03/1919	31/03/1919
Heading	12th R Sco Fus April & May 1919		
War Diary	St Omer	01/04/1919	21/05/1919

WO/95/2366/3

12 Battalion Royal Scots Fusiliers

31ST DIVISION
94TH INFY BDE.

12TH BN ROY. SCOTS FUS.
(AYR&LANARK YEO BN)

MAY ~~JAN~~ 1918-MAY 1919

FROM EGYPT 74 DIV 229 BDE

ATTACHED { 74TH DIVISION
229TH INFY BDE

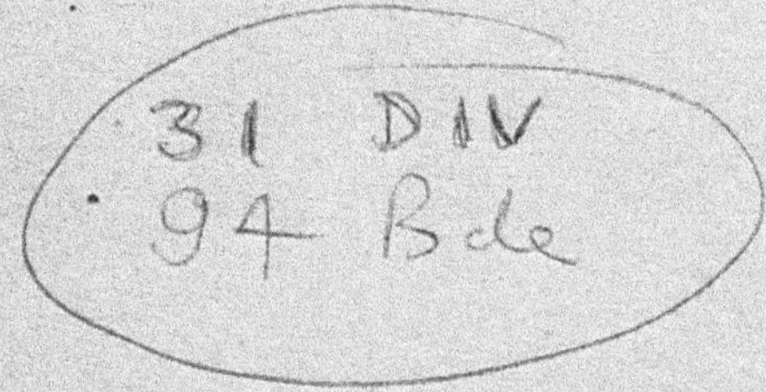

12TH BN ROY. SCOTS FUS.

MAY 1918

FROM EGYPT

12th (Yeo) Bn. R.S.F.

Army Form C. 2118.

229/74 May 1918

12 R S Fus

Vol 2

Instructions regarding War Diaries and Intelligence Summaries are contained in F. S. Regs., Part II. and the Staff Manual respectively. Title pages will be prepared in manuscript.

WAR DIARY
or
~~INTELLIGENCE SUMMARY.~~
(Erase heading not required.)

Place	Date	Hour	Summary of Events and Information	Remarks and references to Appendices
	1st		The Battalion on board the H.M.T. KAISAR-I-HIND, sailed from ALEXANDRIA, EGYPT.	WTRN.
	2nd to 6th		At Sea.	WTRN.
	7th		The Ship arrived at MARSEILLES about 6 AM. The Battn commenced to disembark about 11 30 A.M. When disembarkation was complete the Battn. marched to No 8 REST CAMP where it remained for the night.	WTRN.
	8th		The Battn marched to the station and entrained about 8 30 A.M.	WTRN.
	9th		The day was spent in the train.	WTRN.
	10th		The day was spent in the train.	WTRN.
	11th		The train arrived at NOYELLES in the early morning, and the Battn. immediately detrained and marched to a Staging Camp. The Battn. left NOYELLES and marched to RUE (SOMME) where it was accomodated in a Staging Camp. The Battn. Transport Section was awaiting the Battn. in this Camp and joined up on its arrival.	WTRN.
	12th to 20th		The Battn. remained at RUE. During this period the various alterations in the Establishment were carried out. Specialist training was carried on.	WTRN.
	21st		The Battn. entrained at RUE Station in the early morning and trained to LIGNY-ST-FLOCHEL. The Battn marched from LIGNY-ST. FLOCHEL to COULLEMONT where it was accomodated in Billets.	WTRN.
	22nd to 26th		The Battn. remained at COULLEMONT. Training was carried on here.	WTRN.

12 D 3 Sheet

Instructions regarding War Diaries and Intelligence Summaries are contained in F. S. Regs., Part II. and the Staff Manual respectively. Title pages will be prepared in manuscript.

WAR DIARY
or
INTELLIGENCE SUMMARY.
(*Erase heading not required.*)

Army Form C. 2118.

Place	Date	Hour	Summary of Events and Information	Remarks and references to Appendices
	25th		The Battn. marched from COULLEMONT to GRAND RULLECOURT where it was accomodated in billets.	WTRH.
	26th		The Battn. at GRAND RULLECOURT.	WTRH.
	27th		The Battn. was inspected by Major. General E.S. GIRDWOOD, Comdg 74th (Yeo) DIVISION, who complimented the C.O. on the smart appearance of the Battn.	WTRH.
	28th to 31st		The Battn. remained at GRAND RULLECOURT. The various branches of Specialist Training were carried on here.	WTRH.

W. T. R. Houldsworth.
Lieut.-Colonel.
Comdg. 12th (Yeo) Bn. R.S.F.

D. D. & L., London, E.C.
(A8004) Wt W1771/M2031 750,000 5/17 Sch. 52 Forms/C2118/14

12th R Scots Fus.

June
1918

CONFIDENTIAL.

WAR DIARY

OF

THE 12TH (AYR & LANARK YEOMANRY BATTALION) R. S. F.

JUNE, 1918.

Period : From June 1st, 1918,
To June 30th, 1918.

12th Bn. R. S F

Instructions regarding War Diaries and Intelligence Summaries are contained in F. S. Regs., Part II. and the Staff Manual respectively. Title pages will be prepared in manuscript.

WAR DIARY June 1917
or
~~INTELLIGENCE SUMMARY.~~
(Erase heading not required.)

Army Form C. 2118.

Place	Date	Hour	Summary of Events and Information	Remarks and references to Appendices
In the Field	1st June to 20th		The Battn at GRANDE RULLECOURT. The various branches of Specialist Training were carried on. (Ref map LENS Sheet 11)	WTRH
	21st		The Battn received orders to move to the 31st DIVISION AREA for the purpose of forming part of a new brigade. The Battn marched to TINQUES and entrained for BLARINGHEM arriving there at 4 P.M. The 94th BRIGADE was formed here and was composed of :- 12th BN NORFOLK REGT 12th BN ROYAL SCOTS FUS and 12th BN. ROYAL WELSH FUS.	WTRH
	22nd & 23rd		The Battn remained at BLARINGHEM. (Ref map FRANCE Sheet 36A N W 1:20,000)	WTRH WTRH
	24th		The Battn marched to the Divisional Reserve Area between MORBECQUE and GRAND HASARD and relieved the 1st Bn ROY DUBLIN FUS. (Ref map FRANCE Sheet 36A N.E)	WTRH
	25th		The 94th BDE moved to take over the Sector of the line held by the 92nd BDE this Battn relieving the 11th BN. EAST YORKS REGT.	WTRH
	26th & 27		The Battalion continued to hold this Sector of the Line. On the night of the 27th the Battalion was placed at the disposal of the G.O.C 92nd BDE for Operations.	W.T.R.H.
	28th		In the early morning troops of the 92nd BDE passed through our line to attack and the 4 Coys of this unit manned the Support Line, two Coys holding the Left Battn Sector and two Coys holding the Right Battn Sector.	W.T.R.H.
	29th & 30th		The Battn Disposition remained as on the 28th	WTRH.

W.T.R. Houldsworth
Lieut Colonel
Comdg 12th Bn R.S.F.

(A7092). Wt. W12839/M1293. 750,000. 1/17. D. D. & L., Ltd. Forms/C.2118/14.

Instructions regarding War Diaries and Intelligence Summaries are contained in F. S. Regs., Part II. and the Staff Manual respectively. Title pages will be prepared in manuscript.

WAR DIARY
or
INTELLIGENCE SUMMARY.
(Erase heading not required.)

Army Form C. 2118.

Place	Date	Hour	Summary of Events and Information	Remarks and references to Appendices

Casualties

Killed

295323 Pte WYPER W }
296314 " FINLAY W } Killed in Action 30.6.18.
296238 MARLEY E }
295364 " McCREADIE J }

Died of Wounds

30043 Pte BOAG T Died of Wounds 28.6.18

Wounded

295194	Sgt.	RICHMOND	M.	296045	Cpl	ROXBURGH.	W
11016	Pte	GRIEVE	A	295404	Pte	ANDREW	J.
200263	"	KIRK	R.	295465	"	GILLIES	T.

2/Lieut A MACTAVISH Seaforth Highr.

30269	Pte	McDIMES	W	295434	Pte	TANNOCK	H.
296318	"	HOSE	J.	296266	"	TIBBY	F.
295375	"	STEELE	J.	24419	"	HUTCHISON	C.
295342	"	MURDOCH.	A.	33200	"	CHAPLOW	A

Wounded Shell Gas.

295802	Pte	MILLIGAN	R	296082	Pte	CAMPBELL	J.
29926	"	STEWART	J	295300	"	WILSON	R.
296894	"	MITCHELL	C. E	295305	L/Cpl	CASSIDY	W
32458	"	NOLAN	E	296050	Pte	McINTYRE	T. F.
295942	"	BLAIN	J.	295880	"	FORBES	W G
296255	"	BINGHAM	A	11491	"	GREEN	W
14495	"	DAVIDSON	J.				

W. T. R. Houldsworth
Lieut Colonel
Comdg 12th Bn R.S.F.

2353 Wt. W2544/1454 700,000 5/15 D. D. & L. A.D.S.S./Forms/C. 2118.

94/31.

War Diary
of
12th Bn. R. Scots Fus.
for
July 1918.

CONFIDENTIAL.

94/31

14 D 8 sheet

W A R D I A R Y.

12TH (AYR & LANARK YEOMANRY) BATTALION ROYAL SCOTS FUSILIERS.

JULY - 1918.

VOLUME 2

PERIOD : From July 1st, 1918,
To July 31st, 1918.

Instructions regarding War Diaries and Intelligence Summaries are contained in F. S. Regs., Part II. and the Staff Manual respectively. Title pages will be prepared in manuscript.

WAR DIARY

~~or~~

~~INTELLIGENCE SUMMARY.~~

(Erase heading not required.)

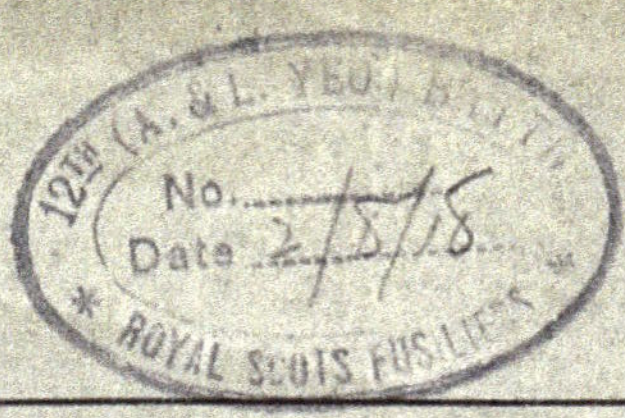

Army Form C. 2118.

Place	Date	Hour	Summary of Events and Information	Remarks and references to Appendices
MAP REF SHEET No 36[A] NE.				
Field	1.7.18		The Battalion moved up to the line in the neighbourhood of LE CORNET PERDU (K 5d.) and relieved the 11th BN E. YORKSHIRE REGT. in the Right Subsector of the Right Brigade Sector.	
"	2.7.18 to 3.7.18		The Battalion held the above Sector with "B" and "C" Companies in the line and "A" and "B" Companies in Support. There were no incidents of importance during this Tour.	
"	3.7.18		The Battalion was relieved by the 12th Bn. Norfolk Regt. and moved into Brigade Reserve in the FORET DE NIEPPE (E 19 C.)	
"	7.7.18		The Battalion moved up to the LEFT Sub Section of the Right Brigade Subsector (E 29) and relieved the 24th BN. R.W.F. During this Tour strong Patrols were sent out to clear the West Bank of the PLATE BECQUE. Strong opposition was encountered from enemy Machine Guns and several attempts to blow up the bridge at E30 a. 4.4 were not successful. The B.G.C. complimented the Battalion on its patrol work which though not successful in clearing the ground was the source of valuable information.	
"	10.7.18		The Battalion was relieved in the Right Brigade Sector by the 93rd Brigade and moved into Divisional Reserve in the neighbourhood of MORBECQUE. This Battalion Camp was at D.20 b.	
"	11.7.18		Companies Bathed and generally cleaning up.	
"	12.7.18		The B.G.C. 94th Brigade inspected the Battalion and witnessed a MARCH PAST in column of Platoons.	
"	13.7.18		Brigade Church Parade in the neighbourhood of GRAND HASARD. The G.O.C. XV Corps, Lieut. General SIR BEAUVOIR DE LISLE inspected the Brigade which marched past in Column of Route. The parade Service followed and was attended by G.O.C. XV CORPS, GOC. 31st Division and B.G.C. 94th Brigade.	
"	14.7.18 to 16.7.18		Training was carried on and instruction in Entrenching and Wiring given by R.E.	
"	16.7.18		The Brigade moved into the Left Brigade Sector. This Battalion relieved the 11th BN EAST LANCS. REGT. in the Right Sub Sector in the neighbourhood of SWARTENBROUCH, E 14 d, with the advance Companies in E 22 d. Patrolling was carried on.	
"	19.7.18		At 7 am. in conjunction with the 93rd Brigade in the Right Sector "C" Company moved forward to the line of the BECQUE and established 2 Posts there. Owing to heavy Machine Gun enfilade fire the 93rd Brigade were ordered to withdraw to their original line and orders were issued to "C" Company to withdraw after dark. This was successfully done and the old line reoccupied.	
"	20.7.18		The Battalion was relieved by the 12th BN NORFOLK REGT. and moved into Brigade Reserve in the neighbourhood of E 7. and D. 6. Working parties were supplied for work under D. Company K.O.Y.L.I. Pioneer Battn. each night on Z Line. From here MAJOR J.C KENNEDY went to ENGLAND and LIEUT COLONEL J.L.A. MACDONALD D.S.O. assumed Command of the Battalion.	

(A7092). Wt. W12839/M1293/ 750,000. 1/17. D. D. & L., Ltd. Forms/C.2118/14

Instructions regarding War Diaries and Intelligence Summaries are contained in F. S. Regs., Part II. and the Staff Manual respectively. Title pages will be prepared in manuscript.

WAR DIARY *Continued*

~~or~~

~~INTELLIGENCE SUMMARY.~~

(Erase heading not required.)

Army Form C. 2118.

Place	Date	Hour	Summary of Events and Information	Remarks and references to Appendices
MAP REF. SHEET	No36A	N.E		
Field	24.7.18.		The Battalion moved up to the Left Sub-Sector of the Left Brigade Sector and relieved the 24TH Bn. R.W.F. Patrols were sent out by day and night and useful information gained.	[illegible]
"	26.7.18		An enemy Raid was attempted against 2 posts held by "C" Company but was beaten off with loss. An identification was obtained from a dead German. (Prussian).	[illegible]
"	28.7.18.		The Brigade was relieved by the 93rd Brigade in the Left Brigade Sector and the Battalion moved to YEOMANRY CAMP D20.	[illegible]
"	29.7.18		Baths and cleaning up.	
"	30.7.18.		Baths and cleaning up. The Commanding Officer inspected the Battn. in the afternoon and instruction was given in the duties of Guard Mounting.	
"	31.7.18.		Training was continued.	[illegible]

Casualties

KILLED	10 O.R.	
DIED of WOUNDS	2 OR.	
WOUNDED.	31 OR.	1 OFFICER. (2/Lieut. WATSON.R.E. 4TH SEAFORTHS. 23.7.18).
MISSING.	3 OR.	
WOUNDED REMAINING ON DUTY	9 OR.	
do.		1 OFFICER. (2/Lieut. INGLIS A.M. 4TH R.S.F. 19.7.18).

J. A. Macdonald Lt. Col.
Commanding 12th Yeo. Battn. Royal Scots Fus.

(A7092). Wt. W12839/M1293. 750,000. 1/17. D. D. & L., Ltd. Forms/C.2118/14

CONFIDENTIAL.

15 P
7 sheets
94/31

986

WAR DIARY

12TH (AYR & LANARK YEOMANRY) BN. R. SCOTS FUSILIERS.

AUGUST, 1918.

VOLUME III

PERIOD:— AUGUST 1ST, 1918.
To
AUGUST 31ST, 1918.

Instructions regarding War Diaries and Intelligence Summaries are contained in F. S. Regs., Part II. and the Staff Manual respectively. Title pages will be prepared in manuscript.

WAR DIARY
or
~~INTELLIGENCE SUMMARY.~~
(Erase heading not required.)

Army Form C. 21

Hour, Date, Place	Summary of Events and Information	Remarks and references to Appendices
1st August. MORBECQUE (SHEET 36A NE)	BATTN in rest, training cleaning and refitting carried on, BRIGADIER'S inspection.	[illegible]
2nd Do Do Do	training continued.	
3rd Do Do Do		
4th Do IN SUPPORT	training continued in the morning, the Battn took over from the 13th YORK & LANCS in support.	[illegible]
5th Do Do Do	WORK on SUPPORT positions carried out, and working party on Z line (BATTN HQRS. at D6d 0.8.	
6th Do Do Do	" " " " " " " " Z "	[illegible]
7 Do Do Do	" " " " " " " " Z "	
8 Do Do Do	" " " " " " " " Z "	
	Usual work done. 1 Officer and 15 O.R's went out on PATROL with 1 offr 12 O.R's of the 8th R.I.R. Patrol left E 23 d 05.90 at 3.15 A.M. They reached E 23 B 0.5. and were heavily fired on, several other ENEMY Posts opened fire also M.G in E 23 b 95.05 this post was attacked by the patrol, the post retired leaving 1 prisoner in our hands. The patrol returned to the same point as of exit. Lt THOMSON & 3 O.R. were wounded.	[illegible]
	A & B Coys went up to the Z line to allow the 2 Coys of the R.W.F. in Z line to go forward while the front line was advanced. A & B Coys returned to GRANDE MARQUETTE FARM at 5 A.M. on the 9th	
9th August IN SUPPORT	Usual WORKING parties supplied. Lt Col. MACDONALD left the Battn. Major TURNER assumed command.	[illegible]
10th Do Do	" " " " to work on Z line.	[illegible]
11th Do Do	The ARTILLERY was active on both sides than usual. The BATTN relieved the 24th R.W.F in the front line on the night of the 11th/12th, A & B Coys being in front in E 17 a & E 18 c. on the LEFT The relief was complete at 1.20 AM. During the relief orders were received that the line was to be advanced to E 18 b 3.7 & E 14 b 9.0. posts to be established there on and prepared for all round defence.	[illegible]
12th Do IN FRONT LINE	This line having been gained, orders were then received to Establish the general line E 18 b 3.4 – E 18 Central – E 24 a 29.99 – E 23 central. This entailed operating on the front of the BDE on our RIGHT. after strong resistance this line was established, except that it bent round an enemy post at E 18 Central, by 4 p.m. A & D Coy had been used for these operations their place in Z line was taken over by a Coy of the 12th NORFOLKS. As the front line was now considered to be too long to be held by one Battn. the 10th EAST YORKS took over the post between E 23 Central and Road at E 18 c 1.1. The relief of these posts was completed by 11.30 pm.	[illegible]
13th Do Do Do	ORDERS were then received to push forward the line to run through LA BECQUE at E 24 a 5.2 – E 24 a 9.8 – E 18 c 1.4 and to NORTHERN BOUNDARY E 18 b 3.7. EAST YORKS to be responsible for the WEST side of the Road. All objectives were taken.	See attached Copy of Report (12th & 13th August) [illegible]
14th Do Do Do	At DAWN the enemy shelled our posts & the rear with GAS shells this was followed by a heavy BARRAGE lasting for 15 minutes the enemy then attacked in extended order, the support platoon was brought up, & the enemy beaten off with losses caused by our Rifle & Lewis gun fire, & by the artillery support which had been called for. On retiring the enemy established their post at E 18 D 0.9.	[illegible]

(9 29 6) W 4141—463 100,000 9/14 H W V Forms/C. 2118/10

Army Form C. 2118.

Instructions regarding War Diaries and Intelligence Summaries are contained in F. S. Regs., Part II. and the Staff Manual respectively. Title pages will be prepared in manuscript.

WAR DIARY
or
~~INTELLIGENCE SUMMARY.~~

(Erase heading not required.)

Place	Date	Hour	Summary of Events and Information	Remarks and references to Appendices
In Front Line	14th August (Cont.)		No further attempt was made by the enemy that day. The ENEMY bombarded the VILLAGE and posts at intervals during the day and night of the 14/15th. YELLOW CROSS, PHOSGENE & LACHRYMATORY shells also being used.	
Do	15 Do		The enemy made repeated attempts to establish M.G. post near our line but these were frustrated by our patrols	
	15 Do		The Battn was relieved by the NORFOLK REGt on the night of the 15/16. The Battn going back into reserve. The relief was complete by 1.30 AM.	
In Support	16 Do		The Battn rested.	
Do	17 Do		100 men supplied in morning and afternoon to work on Z line.	
Do	18 Do		100 " " " morning to work on Z line. 'D' Coy took over from a Coy of NORFOLKS in Z line. During the night of the 18/19th C Coy took over from the left Coy of the NORFOLKS in the front line. D Coy moved up to the trenches in E16B and A & B Coys moved up to the Z line. All Coys were in position by 2.30 AM.	
Do	19 Do		During the NORFOLK advance one platoon from C Coy had to mop up a post and in doing so suffered 10 casualties. C Coy was relieved by a Coy from the R.W.F. on the night of 19/20th and returned to Z line. A Coy were carrying rations & R.E. material to the front line during the night 19/20 & when finished returned to GRANDE MARQUETTE Fm. B Coy were relieved by the R.W.F. & came back to D6.	
Do	20 Do		Reorganising & cleaning. C Coy was relieved from Z line during the night 20/21 by NORFOLKS & came back to GRANDE MARQUETTE Fm. Detailed to GRANDE SEC BOIS	
Do	21 Do		on the night of the 21st. A Coy had a burying party out. During the night of the 21/22 the Battn was relieved by the NORFOLKS & went back to rest at WALLON CAPPELL.	
Wallon Cappell	22 Do		The Battn reorganised and BATHED at LE ROMARIN.	
Do Do	23 Do		The Battn moved in the evening to V.12 B 9.9 arriving there at 11 pm.	
V 12 B 9.9	24 Do		The Battn prepared to take over from the 5th CAMERONS (9th Div.) During the night the BATTN took over the line from the 5th CAMERONS at X22 A 4.2 to X16 C 9.1. The relief was complete by 10.55 pm. H.Qrs at X9D 8.5.	
In Front Line	25 Do		'B' Coy sent a patrol of 1 Off and 20 O.R. at 8 AM. Patrol returned at 10 a.m. Night of the 25/26 wiring party supplied by A & C Coys.	
Do	26 Do		D " supplied wiring party. During the night 26/27 1 N.C.O. & 3 other ranks from 'B' Coy went out as a patrol.	
Do	27 Do		Enemy Artillery very active on BATTN area between 3 and 6 pm. On the night of 27/28 the Battn was relieved, the front line by the 18th DURHAM L.I. H.Qrs and D Coy by the 13th WEST YORKS. The Battn then went into Support to the NORFOLKS. D Coy taking over from the 2nd R.I.R. H.Qrs from the R.W.F. at X3B 4.1. B Coy went into LAUGA Fm. C Coy to SHADOW Hse. Relief was complete at 2 a.m.	
In Support	28th Do		3 Coys on WORKING Party on night of 28/29th.	
Do	29 Do		Working Parties for R.E. to work on Z line	
Divisional Reserve	30th Do		Battn withdrawn to reserve X.3 & 3.C. Working party unloading time at FLETRE.	
	31st Do		Divisional Reserve X.3 & 3.C. Battn working on main METEREN ROAD.	

(A7092). Wt. W12839/M1293. 750,000. 1/17. D. D. & L., Ltd. Forms/C.2118/14.

1/9/18

[signature] Major
Comdg 12th (S.) Bn R.S.F.

REPORT ON OPERATIONS 12th to 15th AUGUST, 1918, RESULTING IN CAPTURE OF VIEUX BERQUIN.

Ref. Map
Sheet 36A N.E. 1/20000.

On the night of the 11th/12th the Battalion was in process of relieving the 24th Battn R.W.F. in the front line of the left Brigade Sector on the general line E 17D 1.4 -- E 17D 5.8 -- E17B 9.0 -- E 17B 9.4 -- E 18A 2.8 -- E 18A 4.9., when orders were received to push out patrols and hold the general line E 18B 3.7 -- E 17B 9.0., on that line being gained and held another general line of advance would be given. This infiltration to be done by pushing forward reconnoitring patrols closely supported by fighting patrols.

As the PLATE BECQUE formed the northern Brigade boundary arrangements were made with the O/C Right Coy of 86th Inf.Bde to allow of a company being formed up on the north side of the BECQUE. O/C "D" Coy was then ordered to rendezvous at E 18c 5.1 (L.P.) and form up by platoons, his left platoon to rest on E 18b 3.7 : each platoon to be formed as a fighting patrol preceded by two small reconnoitring patrols. Distance between rendezvous and left, E 18b 3.7 to be equally divided. Approximately one hour after dawn three platoons were to move echeloned commencing with the left and secure the general line E 18b 3.7 -- E 17b 9.0 : posts established thereon to be prepared for all round defence.

At 5 a.m. the patrols moved off across the BECQUE and a few minutes later the enemy opened rifle and M.G. fire from posts approx. E 18a 9.5 and E 18b 4.5. These posts were engaged by the patrols and garrison killed or captured. Prisoners taken here were 1 Off. and 22 O.R.

At 5-30 a.m. the Company reached the objective and dug in. A large party of the enemy estimated at 50 to 60 were seen about E 18c 9.4. These put up their hands in token of surrender but on approach of our men opened on them with rifle and M.G. fire and then withdrew rapidly.

The first general line having been gained orders were then received to establish by fighting and reconnoitring patrols in the same manner, the general line E 18b 3.7 -- E 18central -- E 24a 20.99 -- E 23central. This entailed operating on thefront of the Bde on the right, arrangements for which were accordingly made. Orders were then issued to the three Companies, "B", right company, "A", centre company, and "D", left company, to send out reconnoitring and fighting patrols to secure this line and consolidate thereon.

The enemy were observed leaving the outskirts of the village and the right company (B) pushed out patrols down the main road to clear the houses and hedges as far as E 18c 1.1. Some resistance was encountered but overcome until within about 200 yards of the objective when an enemy post, estimated strength 50, with M.G., was located. Patrols were then ordered not to advance further but to keep enemy in view. A fighting patrol from the centre company (A) was then ordered to work down east side of main road and approach this enemy post from south-east, the patrols of the right company (B) co-operating. This enemy post was captured and prisoners taken, some of the enemy escaping to the south. Strong posts were then established at E 18c 1.1. The patrols of the right of "B" Company met with heavy M.G. fire but succeeded in overcoming it and clearing the ground well beyond the line E 18c 1.1 -- E 23b 0.6, the line on the right being then advanced to the objective and the posts dug in. The left company (D) had pushed forward posts in conformity but owing to a strong enemy post at E 18central had not got its right as far forward as intended. The centre company (A) had formed a line of posts from E 18c 1.1 linking up with left of "D" Company about E 18c 50.90. The general line ordered was secured by 7 P.M. with exception that it bent round the enemy post at E 18central.

The line now held was then considered too long for the Battalion (E 23central -- E 18b 3.7) and orders were received that the right posts from E 23 central to the main road at E 18c 1.1 would be taken over by the 10th East Yorks. Arrangements were accordingly made and the relief completed by 11-30 P.M., the men withdrawn being utilised to strengthen the line of the centre and left companies and as close support.

Orders were then received that the line was to be pushed forward the following morning in a similar manner in conjunction with East Yorks who were to be responsible for the west side of the main road. The line to be established to run through LA BECQUE E 24a 5.2 -- E 24a 9.8 -- E 18c 8.4 and then on to northern boundary E 18b 3.7. O/C "B" Coy was then ordered to send out fighting patrols to clear the remainder of VIEUX BERQUIN down to E 24a 5.2 and establish posts there, and in conjunction with "A" Coy to push out E 24a 9.8. The patrol ordered to clear the village was held up almost at once, the second attempt was not much more successful, but immediately the patrols moving east to E 24a 9.6 had cleared the ground in their front and reached the objec: tive, the patrol clearing the village was enabled to reach its objective and establish a post at E 24a 5.2. Touch was then gained with the 10th East Yorks and a liaison post established.
The centre company (A) pushed forward its posts to conform with the gen: eral line ordered and thereafter sent out apatrol to clear its front. This patrol proceeded towards the trees at E 18b 8.3 where an enemy post was found and rushed. The post was more strongly held than was supposed and the enemy gave the alarm and M.Gs opened a cross-fire cutting off the patrol. Fromtrenches immediately behind this position the enemy advanced in 2 lines to cut off the patrol and others were seen advancing also. The patrol opened fire and the prisoners obtained in the first instance,taking advantage of this, doubled into the shelters. Men were detailed to bomb these shelters. An effort was made to get the first 2 lines of the enemy to surrender but this was prevented by an enemy Officer rushing up with reinforcements and threatening these men with his revolver. They appeared to gain confidence at his approach and doubled back towards him. Casualties were inflicted on them by our patrol. The Officer in charge of the patrol, seeingthe impossibility of dealing with such a large force of the enemy, (estimated 60), bayonetted the enemy in the shelters and ordered his patrol to scatter through the crops and return to our posts. Several of the patrol were wounded while passing through the M.G. barrage but were got safely in. 6 of the patrol were missing and of these it is known that one was killed in a shelter which was bombed. 2 were seen some time afterwards carrying stretchers for the enemy but owing to the distance it was impossible to identify them. A patrol was sent out later to try and find the missing but no trace of them could be found.

All the objectives on the general line were gained and in accordance with orders the posts on the right at E 24a 5.2 -- E 24a 8.5 -- E 24a 99.60, were taken over by the 10th East Yorks. On relief, the men occupying these posts were withdrawn to support.

At dawn on the 14th what appeared to be enemy patrols were observed on the front of the centre and left companies about 200 yards off. Later, these increased and were estimated at 80 men with M.Gs about the same time the enemy put a number of gas shells in the vicinity of the posts all along the line and in rear. This was followed by a heavy barrage of 15 minutes duration over the same area. The enemy then attempted an attack on our posts in extended order, making much noise. A platoon was called up from the supports and together with the front posts engaged the enemy with rifle and L.G. fire. The attack was brought to a standstill and then gradually fell back. Artillery support was called for and promptly given. Casualties were inflicted on the enemy by our rifles,L.G.,and artillery fire. On returning the enemy again established their post at E 18d 0.9 which gave some trouble by sniping.

No further attempt was made by the enemy that day. The enemy bambarded the village and posts at intervals during the day and ni[illegible] of the 14th/15th, with harassingfire, yellow cross, phosgene and lachrymatory shells also being used.

On the 15th inst. the enemy made repeated attempts to establish M.G. posts near our line but on every occasion these were frustrated by our p atrols. Latterly the enemy gave up these attempts but continued sniping from the one post only at E 18d 0.9.

The Battalion wasrelieved by the 12th Batt. Norfolk Regt. on the night of 15th/16th.

[illegible signature]

Major,
Comdg. 12th (Y.eo.) Batt. R.S.F.

1/9/18.

12 R. Scots Fus

Sept
1918

<u>Confidential</u>

War Diary

of

12th (Yeo) Bn Royal Scots Fusiliers

from 1st September 1918 to 30th September 1918

(Volume IV)

Instructions regarding War Diaries and Intelligence Summaries are contained in F. S. Regs., Part II. and the Staff Manual respectively. Title pages will be prepared in manuscript.

WAR DIARY
or
INTELLIGENCE SUMMARY.

(Erase heading not required.)

Army Form C. 2118.

Place	Date	Hour	Summary of Events and Information	Remarks and references to Appendices
Divisional Reserve Area FONTAINE HOUCK	September		Reserve area X 3 b 3.0 Batn. ordered to move forward left X 3 b 3.0 at 4-30 p.m marched towards BAILLEUL orders cancelled on line of march returning to X 3 b 3.0 about 7-30 p.m.	
	2nd 3rd		Divisional reserve area.	
	4th		Batn left X 3 b 3.0. 9.30 a.m marched through BAILLEUL arriving S.15 a.7.4. at midday rested till 7.30 p.m continued march forward arriving NAB LINES T.23.c.8.8. (Batn in support.	
	5th		Batn in support T.28 c.3.8.	
	6th		94th Bde relieved 31st Bde. Batn in front line. L boundary HYDE PARK CORNER U.19.b.4.7 R boundary PLOEGSTEERT U.25.D.4.b. Batn H.Q. PETIT MONQUE FARM T.28.D.8.8.	
	7 & 8th		Batn in PLOEGSTEERT area.	
	8/9th		Batn relieved by 12th NORFOLK REGT.	
	9th		Batn in reserve S.23.a.5.4.	
	10th		Lt Col [illegible] CMG. DSO. assumed command	
	11/12th		Batn in reserve. 94th relieved by 92nd Bde	
	13th/14th		94th Bde in reserve.	
	18/19th		12th R.S.F. relieved 12th York & Lancs in B10.a.2.3. L. front boundary. B.1.C.A. front boundary. B.17. central.	
	19/24th		Batn in line Right sector. "B" Coy H.Q. blown in by trench mortar. 23rd Major Turner took over command.	
Bde Rest.	24/25th		Batn relieved by 10th East Yorks marched from line to BAILLEUL entrained 3.30 a.m.	
do	26th		Bde in rest HAZEBROUCK	
	28th		Batn entrained at HAZEBROUCK arriving at BAILLEUL 10.31 a.m. marched to reserve area. Batn ordered to move forward leaving at 10.30 p.m. attached 92nd Bde. 2 Coys in the line HYDE PARK CORNER.	
attached 92nd Bde	29th		Batn H.Q. at HYDE PARK CORNER 2 coys moved forward N. of HYDE PARK CORNER 2 coys in NIEPPE system 1 coy detailed to form chain of posts on left of 10th East Yorks about U.15.a.8.8. This coy detailed to form chain of posts U.15.D.9.7. to U.22.C.5.6. all objectives gained without loss. Instruction given to withdraw this coy. Batn assembled on a line U.15.D.9.6. to U.5.b.8.9.9. Batn ordered to push forward & make good the line of RIVER LYS. U.23.b.7.5. to U.17.b.9.6. all objectives gained ~~without~~ casualties slight	
	30th		Batn withdrawn to Bde reserve. H.Q. PETIT MONQUE FARM. Withdrawn from 92nd Bde. Batn ordered to move back to 94th Bde Reserve at S.23.a.5.4.	

J R Turner
Major
Cmdg 12th [illegible]

2353 Wt. W2544/1454 700,000 5/15 D. D. & L. A.D.S.S./Forms/C. 2118.

17.P. Ashele

Confidential

Vol 11

War Diary
of
12th (Yeo) Bn R.S.F.
for
Month of October 1918.

Volume 5.

Army Form C. 2118.

Instructions regarding War Diaries and Intelligence Summaries are contained in F. S. Regs., Part II. and the Staff Manual respectively. Title pages will be prepared in manuscript.

WAR DIARY
or
INTELLIGENCE SUMMARY.
(*Erase heading not required.*)

Place	Date	Hour	Summary of Events and Information	Remarks and references to Appendices
94th Bde in Reserve.	October 1st to 6th		Batn in reserve at S.23 a.8.5.	H.a.P.
94th Bde relieved the 93rd in the Line	6/7th		Night of 6th/7th 12th R.S.F. Relieved the 18th D.L.I. in the Line (WARNETON to GRANGER'S COTTAGE. U.23.c.) Batn H.Q. U.16.b.	H.a.P.
	7th 8th 9th		Batn in the Line.	H.a.P.
			Night of the 9/10th Batn relieved by the 24th R.W.F.	H.a.P.
	10th		Batn in Reserve. (Area T.24. & U.19.)	H.a.P.
	11th		" " " "	
	12th		Afternoon of the 12th Batn relieved by the 11th Bn E. YORKS REGT moved back to reserve camp S.23.b.8.5	H.a.P.
94th Bde in Reserve	to 15th		Batn in reserve at S.23.b.8.5.	H.a.P.
	16th		Moved forward to ALDERSHOT CAMP (T.19.)	H.a.P.
	17th		" " " WARNETON.	H.a.P.
	18th		"	H.a.P.
	19th		"	H.a.P.
	20th		Moved forward to LANNOY. Line of march through QUESNOY. WAMBRECHIES & CROIX.	H.a.P.
	to 24th		Bde in Reserve at LANNOY.	H.a.P.

Instructions regarding War Diaries and Intelligence Summaries are contained in F. S. Regs., Part II. and the Staff Manual respectively. Title pages will be prepared in manuscript.

WAR DIARY
or
INTELLIGENCE SUMMARY.

(Erase heading not required.)

Page (2).

Army Form C. 2118.

Place	Date	Hour	Summary of Events and Information	Remarks and references to Appendices
Field	25/10/18		The Battn. marched to MOUSCRON (Sheet TOURNAI 5) and billeted there for the night.	H.a.P.
	26/10/18		The Battn. marched to STACEGHEM and billeted there for the night.	H.a.P.
	27/10/18		The 94th (Y) Inf Bde moved into the Support Area, the Battn marching to the village of DEERLYCK, where billets were occupied.	H.a.P. H.a.P.
	28/10/18		The Battn remained at DEERLYCK. Training was carried on.	H.a.P.
	29/10/18		At night the Battn moved forward, taking over the Line from the 11th Bn. E. LANCS REGT. Approx. J. 34.c. 5.00. to P.4.c.4.5.	H.a.P.
	30/10/18		Batt. in Line.	H.a.P.
	31/10/18		Attack carried out in conjunction with 34th Div. on left of Battn. & 35th Division on right. Objective HOLENDRIES. N. to J. 36.c. 7.7, S. to P.6.c.6.4. All objectives gained in spite of heavy Machine Gun fire. Our casualties were comparatively slight. Material captured – 3 field guns. Prisoners captured – 605.	H.a.P.

H.a. Pollock Major
for Lieut Colonel
Comdg 12th (Y) Bn R.S.F.

GR/4
3/11/18

A7092). Wt. W12839/M1297 750,000. 1/17. D. D & L., Ltd. Forms/C2118/14.

94/31

War Diary
of
12th (Yeo) Bn,
Royal Scots Fus.,
for
November 1918.

1st Copy

M/02

THE GALLIPOLI CAMPAIGN.

VOL II

CHAPTER XX

The Landing at Suvla

July 1931

Instructions regarding War Diaries and Intelligence Summaries are contained in F. S. Regs., Part II. and the Staff Manual respectively. Title pages will be prepared in manuscript.

WAR DIARY
or
INTELLIGENCE SUMMARY.
(Erase heading not required.)

Army Form C. 2118.

Place	Date	Hour	Summary of Events and Information	Remarks and references to Appendices
Field	31-10-18		The attack was continued to the second objective on the general line SMEIER - CASTER and a line of posts established through K32 central - Q2 central (Ref Map Sheet 29. 1/40,000) Considerable opposition was experienced at the commencement of the second phase but was overcome.	
	1-11-18		Orders were received for the advance to be continued by fighting patrols to the general line KLOESTERHOEK KWAADESTRAAT. Patrols were sent out, the enemy offered little opposition and the line was gained without loss. The patrols were again pushed forward through ELSEGHEM towards DRIESCH. At this point the French troops crossed the front of the patrols and took up posts along the SCHELDT. It was then ascertained that the French would hold the ground gained and the Battalion was then withdrawn. The Battalion was then closed and marched back to billets in VEERKE.	
	2nd		The Battn marched to COURTRAI and billeted there for the night	
	3rd		The Battn. marched to LAUWE where billets were occupied	
	4th to 9th		Battalion Training at LAUWE.	
	10th		The Battn. marched to AVELGHEM and billeted there for the night	
	11th		The Battn marched to RENAIX and billets occupied	
	12th		Battn. at RENAIX	
	13th		Battn marched to AMOUGIES and billeted there for the night	
	14th		Battn marched to ST LOUIS and billeted there for the night	
	15th		Battn marched to LAUWE where billets were occupied	
	16th to 21st		Battn. Training at LAUWE	
	22nd		The Bde was inspected by the Divisional Commander who presented Medal Ribands.	
	23rd		Battn Training at LAUWE.	

A7092). Wt. W12839/M1297 750,000. 1/17. D. D & L., Ltd. Forms/C2118/14.

Instructions regarding War Diaries and Intelligence Summaries are contained in F. S. Regs., Part II. and the Staff Manual respectively. Title pages will be prepared in manuscript.

WAR DIARY
or
INTELLIGENCE SUMMARY.
(Erase heading not required.)

Army Form C. 2118.

Place	Date	Hour	Summary of Events and Information	Remarks and references to Appendices
Field	24.11.18.		Battn marched to MENIN where billets were occupied for the night.	[initials]
	25th		Battn marched to VLAMERTINGHE and billeted there for the night	[initials]
	26th		Battn marched to TERDEGHEM and billeted there for the night	[initials]
	27th		Battn marched to LA CROSSE and billeted there for the night	[initials]
	28th		Battn marched to LONGUENESSE where billets were occupied	[initials]
	29th and 30th		Battn Training at LONGUENESSE	[initials]

12th (A. & L. YEO.) B. ... ROYAL ... FUSILIERS
No.........
Date.........

[signature] Lieut. Col.
Comdg. 12th (Yeo) Bn. R. Scots Fus.

8353 Wt. W2544/1454 700,000 5/15 D. D. & L. A.D.S.S./Forms/C. 2118.

Mr. Daws 19. D.
3 sheets

(6392) Wt. W6192/P875 1,500,000 4/18 McA & W Ltd (E 2815) Forms W3091/4.

Army Form W.3091.

WO 1/3

Cover for Documents.

Confidential

Nature of Enclosures.

War Diary

of

12th (Yeo.) Bn. Royal Scots Fusiliers

from 1st December 1918 to 31st December 1918.

(Volume 7 ~~12~~.)

Notes, or Letters written.

Instructions regarding War Diaries and Intelligence Summaries are contained in F. S. Regs., Part II. and the Staff Manual respectively. Title pages will be prepared in manuscript.

WAR DIARY
or
INTELLIGENCE SUMMARY.
(*Erase heading not required.*)

Army Form C. 2118.

Place	Date	Hour	Summary of Events and Information	Remarks and references to Appendices
	1.12.18. to 16th		Battn at LONGUENESSE (Ref map. Hazebrouck 5a 1/100.000. Salvage work and recreational training carried on.	
	17th		Battn. moved to VAL de LUMBRES Camp (Ref map Hazebrouck 5a 1/100,000.	
	18th to 31st		Battn carrying out Salvage work.	
			Honours & Rewards.	
			295536 Sgt Caldwell J. awarded the Victoria Cross.	
			Military Cross awarded to 6 Officers.	
			Distinguished Conduct Medal awarded to 5 O.R.	
			Military Medal awarded to 47 OR.	
			Bar to Military Medal awarded to 1 OR.	
			Croix De Guerre with Star awarded to 1 Officer.	
			Croix De Guerre Division awarded to 1 OR.	
			Croix De Guerre Brigade awarded to 1 OR.	

[Stamp: 12th ... BATTN. No. Date ROYAL SCOTS FUSILIERS]

[Signature] Lieut. Col.
Comdg. 12th (Yeo) Bn. Royal Scots Fusiliers

D. D. & L., London, E.C. (A7883) Wt W809/M1672 350,000 4/17 Sch. 52a Forms/C/2118/14

20 P
3 sheets

(6392) Wt. W6192/P875 1,500,000 4/18 McA & W Ltd (E 2815) Forms W3091/4.

Army Form W.3091.

Vol 36

Cover for Documents.

Confidential

Nature of Enclosures.

War Diary

of

12th (Yeo) Bn. Royal Scots Fusiliers

from 1st January 1919 to 31st January 1919.

(Volume VIII)

Notes, or Letters written.

31

Instructions regarding War Diaries and Intelligence Summaries are contained in F. S. Regs., Part II. and the Staff Manual respectively. Title pages will be prepared in manuscript.

WAR DIARY
or
INTELLIGENCE SUMMARY.
(Erase heading not required.)

Army Form C. 2118.

Place	Date	Hour	Summary of Events and Information	Remarks and references to Appendices
	1.1.19 to 28th		Battn at VAL de LUMBRES Camp (Ref. map Hazebrouck 5a 1/100000) Salvage work being carried on. JRM	
	15th		Brigadier General Commanding 94th (Yeo) Inf Brigade, presented Medal Ribands to recipients of awards. JRM	
	29th		Battalion moved by rail from ST. OMER to CALAIS for strike duty and occupied camp at COULOGNE JRM	
	30th		Battalion employed guarding Ordnance Dumps. JRM	
	31st		Battalion withdrawn from strike duty and returned by rail from CALAIS to LUMBRES and occupied same camp at Val de Lumbres. JRM	

J R Farmer [illegible]
Cmdg 12 Bn R S F.

D. D. & L., London, E.C.
(A7883) Wt W809/M1672 350,000 4/17 Sch. 52a Forms/C/2118/14

WO 95/1465

21 P
3 sheet

(6392) Wt. W6192/P875 1,500,000 4/18 McA & W Ltd (E 2815) Forms W3091/4. Army Form W.3091.

Cover for Documents.

Confidential

Nature of Enclosures.

War Diary

12th (Yeo) Bn. Royal Scots Fusiliers

From 1st February 1919 to 28th February 1919.

Notes, or Letters written.

Instructions regarding War Diaries and Intelligence Summaries are contained in F. S. Regs., Part II, and the Staff Manual respectively. Title pages will be prepared in manuscript.

WAR DIARY
or
INTELLIGENCE SUMMARY.

(Erase heading not required.)

Army Form C. 2118.

Place	Date	Hour	Summary of Events and Information	Remarks and references to Appendices
	1-2-19 to 5-2-19		Battn. at VAL DE LUMBRES Camp. (Ref map. Hazebrouck 5a 1/100,000.) Salvage work being carried on.	
	6th		Battn. moved by motor Lorries to Fifth Army Staging Camp at HONDEGHEM.	
	7th to 28th		Battn. employed on duties at Staging Camp.	

12th (A. & L. YEO.) BATTN. No. ____ Date ____ ROYAL SCOTS FUSILIERS

J R Murner Lieut. Col.
Comdg. 12th (Yeo.) Bn. R. Scots Fus.

D. D. & L., London, E.C. (A7883) Wt W809/M1672 350,000 4/17 Sch. 52a Forms/C/2118/14

22D
3 [illegible]

(6392) Wt. W6192/P875 1,500,000 4/18 McA & W Ltd (E 2815) Forms W3091/4.

Army Form W.3091.

Cover for Documents.

WO 16

Confidential

Nature of Enclosures.

War Diary

of

12th (Yeo) Bn. Royal Scots Fusiliers

from 1st March 1919 to 31st March 1919

Notes, or Letters written.

Instructions regarding War Diaries and Intelligence Summaries are contained in F. S. Regs., Part II. and the Staff Manual respectively. Title pages will be prepared in manuscript.

WAR DIARY
or
~~INTELLIGENCE SUMMARY.~~
(Erase heading not required.)

Army Form C. 2118.

Place	Date	Hour	Summary of Events and Information	Remarks and references to Appendices
	1-3-19 to 3rd		Battn. at Fifth Army Staging Camp. Hondeghem. (Ref Map Hazebrouck 5a. 1:100000)	
	4th		Battn moved by Motor Lorries to MOIR CAMP, ST. OMER. (Ref Map. St. Omer Sheet 27 1/40,000.)	
	5th to 31st		Battn at MOIR CAMP, ST. OMER	

12TH (A. & L. YEO.) BATTN. No. Date * ROYAL SCOTS FUSILIERS *

J R [illegible] Lieut. Col.
Comdg 12th (Yeo) Bn. Royal Scots Fusiliers

D. D. & L., London, E.C.
(A7883) Wt W809/M1672 350,000 4/17 Sch. 52a Forms/C/2118/14

12th R Sco Fus

April

7

MAY

1919

Instructions regarding War Diaries and Intelligence Summaries are contained in F. S. Regs., Part II. and the Staff Manual respectively. Title pages will be prepared in manuscript.

WAR DIARY
or
INTELLIGENCE SUMMARY.
(Erase heading not required.)

Army Form C. 2118.

12 R Scots Fus

Apl 17

Place	Date	Hour	Summary of Events and Information	Remarks and references to Appendices
St. Omer	1-4-19 to 30-4-19		Battalion at Moir Camp St. Omer (Ref map. St. Omer sheet 24 1/100000)	
			Jas Grant Lt & A/Adjt for OC 12 (Yeo) Bn R S F	

12TH (A. & L. YEO.) BATTN. No. Date ROYAL SCOTS FUSILIERS

D. D. & L., London, E.C. (A7883) Wt W809/M1672 350,000 4/17 Sch. 52a Forms/C/2118/14

23 D

1 dr

Instructions regarding War Diaries and Intelligence Summaries are contained in F. S. Regs., Part II. and the Staff Manual respectively. Title pages will be prepared in manuscript.

WAR DIARY
or
~~INTELLIGENCE SUMMARY.~~
(Erase heading not required.)

12 R S F

Army Form C. 2118.

VOL 18

Place	Date	Hour	Summary of Events and Information	Remarks and references to Appendices
St. Omer	1.5.19 to 16th		Battalion at MOIR CAMP, ST OMER (Reference map St. OMER Sheet 27 1/100000.)	Ceased
	9th		Battn reduced to Cadre strength	
	14th		Battn Cadre moved by motor lorry to WIZERNES	
	18th		Battn Cadre entrained at WIZERNES and arrived DUNKERQUE occupied billets at Hospice Camp	
	19th		Battn Cadre moved to W3 Mardyck Camp	
	21st		Battn Cadre embarked for UK	

12th (A. & L. YEO.) BN. ROYAL SCOTS FUSILIERS * No. Date

J R Turner Lieut. Col.
Comdg. 12 (Yeo) Bn. R. S. F.

24D
1m

D. D. & L., London, E.C.
(A7833) Wt W809/M1672 350,000 4/17 Sch. 52a Forms/C2118/14

www.ingramcontent.com/pod-product-compliance
Lightning Source LLC
Chambersburg PA
CBHW081458160426
43193CB00013B/2523

* 9 7 8 1 4 7 4 5 1 5 8 5 6 *